THE
FAMA FRATERNITATIS
AND
CONFESSION
OF THE
ROSICRUCIAN FRATERNITY

ADAPTED BY

ARTHUR EDWARD WAITE

From Original Translations By
Thomas Vaughan (Eugenius Philalethes)

Stone Guild Publishing
Plano, Texas
http://www.stoneguildpublishing.com/

2009

Originally Published By:
J. W. BOUTON
1888

This Edition Copyright © 2009
Stone Guild Publishing, Inc.
Plano, Texas
http://www.stoneguildpublishing.com/

First Paperback Edition 2009

ISBN-13 978-1-60532-045-8
ISBN-10 1-60532-045-5

10 9 8 7 6 5 4 3 2

ANALYSIS OF CONTENTS.

PAGE

CHAPTER THE FIRST.

The Fama Fraternitatis of the Meritorious Order of the Rosy Cross, addressed to the learned in general and the Governors of Europe 5

CHAPTER THE SECOND.

The Confession of the Rosicrucian Fraternity, addressed to the learned of Europe 29

CHAPTER I.

THE FAMA FRATERNITATIS OF THE MERITORIOUS ORDER OF THE ROSY CROSS, ADDRESSED TO THE LEARNED IN GENERAL, AND THE GOVERNORS OF EUROPE.

THE original edition of the "Universal Reformation" contained the manifesto bearing the above title, but which the notary Haselmeyer declares to have existed in manuscript as early as the year 1610, as would also appear from a passage in the Cassel edition of 1614, the earliest which I have been able to trace. It was reprinted with the "Confessio Fraternitatis" and the "Allgemeine Reformation der Ganzen Welt" at Franckfurt-on-the-Mayne in 1615. A Dutch translation was also published in this year, and by 1617 there had been four Franckfurt editions, the last omitting the "Universal Reformation," which, though it received an elaborate alchemical elucidation by Brotoffer,[1] seems gradually to have dropped out of notice. "Other editions," says Buhle, "followed in the years immediately succeeding, but these it is unnecessary to notice. In the title page of the third Franckfurt edition stands—*First printed at Cassel* in the year 1616. But the four first words apply to the original edition, the four last to this.[2]

[1] "Elucidarius Major, oder Ekleuchterunge über die Reformation der ganzen Weiten Welt. . . .; Durch Radtichs Brotofferr." 1617.
[2] De Quincey, "Rosicrucians and Freemasons."

*To the
Wise and Understanding
Reader*

Wisdom (sayeth Solomon) is a treasure unto men that never faileth, for she is the breath of the power of God and an inherence flowing from the glory of the Almighty; she is the brightness of the everlasting light, the unspotted mirror of the power of God, and the image of His goodness. She teacheth civility with righteousness and strength, she knoweth things of old, and conjectureth aright what is to come; she knoweth the subtleties of speeches and can expound dark sentences; she foreseeth signs and wonders, with the advent of seasons and times. With this treasure was our first father Adam before his fall fully endued; hence it doth appear that after God had brought before him all the creatures of the field and the fowls under the heavens, he gave to everyone of them their proper name, according to their Nature.

Although now, through the sorrowful fall into sin, this excellent jewel wisdom hath been lost, and mere darkness and ignorance is come into the world, yet, notwithstanding, the Lord God hath sometimes hitherto bestowed and made manifest the same to some of his friends; the wise King Solomon doth testify of himself that he upon his earnest prayer and desire obtained such wisdom of God that thereby he knew how the world was made, understood the operation of the elements, the beginning, ending, and middest of the times, the alterations, the days of the turning of the sun, the change of seasons, the circuits of years and the positions of stars, the natures of living creatures and the furies of wild beasts, the violence of winds, the reasoning's of men, the diversities of plants, the virtues of roots, and all such things as are either secret or manifest, them he knew.

Now, I do not think that there can be found anyone who would not wish and desire with all his heart to be partaker of this noble treasure, but seeing the same felicity can happen to none except God Himself give wisdom and send His Holy Spirit from above, we have set forth in print this little treaty, to wit, the *Famam* and *Confessionem* of the Laudable Fraternity of the Rosy Cross, to be read by every one, because in them is clearly shown and discovered what concerning it the world hath hereafter to expect. Although now these things may seem somewhat strange, and many might esteem it to be a philosophical show and no true history which is published and spoken of the Fraternity of the Rosy Cross, it shall therefore sufficiently appear by our Confession that there is more *in recessu* then may be imagined, and it shall also be easily understood and observed by everyone, (yf he be not altogether void of understanding) what now a days is meant thereby.

Those who are true disciples of wisdom and true followers of the spiritual arte will consider better of these things, and have them in greater estimation, as also judge far otherwise of them, as hath been done of some principal persons but especially of Adam Haselmeyer, *Notarius Publicus* to the Archduke Maximilian, who likewise hath made an extract *ex scriptis Theologicis Theophrasti,* and written a treatise under the title Jesuits, wherein he willet that every Christian should be a true Jesuite, that is, should walk, live, and be in Jesus. He was but ill rewarded of the Jesuites, because in his answer written upon the *Famam* he did name those of the Fraternity of the Rosy Cross, "the highly illuminated men and undeceiving Jesuites," for they, not able to brook this, laid hands on him and put him into the gallies, for which they likewise are to expect their reward.

Blessed Aurora will now begin to appear, who (after the passing away of the dark night of Saturn) with her brightness altogether extinguished the shinning of the moon, or the small sparkles of the heavenly wisdom which yet remains with men, and is a fore runner of pleasant Phœbus, who, with her clear and fiery glistening beams, brings forth that blessed day, long wished for of many truehearted, by which daylight then shall truly be known and seen, all heavenly treasures of godly wisdom, as also the secrets of all hidden and invisible things in the world, according to the doctrine of our forefathers and ancient wise men.

This will be the right Kingly Rubie, most excellent shining Carbuncle, of the which it is said that he doth shine and give light in darkens, and is a perfect medicine of all imperfect metaline bodies, to change them into the best gold and to cure all diseases of men, easing them of their pains and miseries.

Be therefore gentle reader admonished, that with me you do earnestly pray to God, that it may please Him to open the harts and ears of all ill-hearing people, and to grant unto them His blessing, that they may be able to know Him in His omnipotence, with admiring contemplation of Nature, to His honor and praise, and to the love, help, comfort, and strengthening of our neighbors, and to the restoring of health of all the diseased. Amen.

Fama Fraternitatis; or, a Discovery of the Fraternity of the most Laudable Order of the Rosy Cross.

Seeing the only wise and merciful God in these latter days hath poured out so richly His mercy and goodness to mankind, whereby we do attain more and more to the perfect knowledge of His Son Jesus Christ and of Nature, that justly we may boast of the happy time wherein there is not only discovered unto us the half part of the world, which was heretofore unknown and hidden, but He hath also made manifest unto us many wonderful and never-heretofore seen works and creatures of Nature, and, moreover, hath raised men, endued with great wisdom, which might partly renew and reduce all arts (in this our spotted and imperfect age) to perfection, so that finally man might thereby understand his own nobleness and worth, and why he is called *Microcosmus,* and how far his knowledge extended in Nature.

Although the rude world herewith will be but little pleased, but rather smile and scoff thereat; also the pride and covetousness of the learned is so great, it will not suffer them to agree together; but were they united, they might, out of all those things which in this our age God doth so richly bestow on us, collect *Librum Naturæ,* or, a Perfect Method of all Arts. But such is their opposition that they still keep, and are loath to leave, the old course, esteeming Porphyry, Aristotle, and Galen, yea, and that which hath but a mere show of learning, more than the clear and manifested Light and Truth. Those, if they were now living, with much joy would leave their erroneous doctrines; but here is too great weakness for such a great work. And although in Theology, Physic, and the Mathematic, the truth doth oppose it itself, nevertheless, the old Enemy, by his subtlety and craft, doth show himself in hindering every good purpose by his instruments and contentious wavering people.

To such an intention of a general reformation, the most godly and highly-illuminated Father, our Brother, C. R. C., a German, the chief and original of our Fraternity, hath much and long time labored, who, by reason of his poverty (although descended of noble parents), in the fifth year of his age was placed in a cloister, where he had learned indifferently the Greek and Latin tongues, and (upon his earnest desire and request), being yet in his growing years, was associated to a Brother, P. A. L., who had determined to go to the Holy Land. Although this Brother dyed in Cyprus, and so never came to Jerusalem, yet our Brother C. R. C. did not return, but shipped himself over, and went to Damasco, minding from thence to go to Jerusalem. However, because of the feebleness of his body he remained there, and by his skill in physic he obtained much favor with the Turks, and in the meantime he became acquainted with the Wise Men of Damcar in Arabia, and beheld what great wonders they wrought, and how Nature was discovered unto them.

Hereby was that high and noble spirit of Brother C. R. C. so stirred up, that Jerusalem was not so much now in his mind as Damasco;[1] also he could not bridle his desires any longer, but made a bargain with the Arabians that they should carry him for a certain sum of money to Damcar.

---

[1] Damascus and the unknown city denominated Damcar are continually confused in the German editions. Brother C. R. C. evidently did not project a journey to Damascus, which he had already reached; nevertheless this is the name appearing in this place, and I have decided on retaining it for reasons which will subsequently be made evident.

He was but of the age of sixteen years when he came thither, yet of a strong Dutch constitution. There the Wise Men received him not as a stranger (as he himself witnessed), but as one whom they had long expected; they called him by his name, and showed him other secrets out of his cloister, whereat he could not but mightily wonder.

He learned there better the Arabian tongue, so that the year following he translated the book M into good Latin, which he afterwards brought with him. This is the place where he did learn his Physic and his Mathematics, whereof the world hath much cause to rejoice, if there were more love and less envy.

After three years he returned again with good consent, shipped himself over *Sinus Arabicus* into Egypt, where he remained not long, but only took better notice there of the plants and creatures. He sailed over the whole Mediterranean Sea for to come unto Fez, where the Arabians had directed him.

It is a great shame unto us that wise men, so far remote the one from the other, should not only be of one opinion, hating all contentious writings, but also be so willing and ready, under the seal of secrecy, to impart their secrets to others. Every year the Arabians and Africans do send one to another, inquiring one of another out of their arts, if happily they had found out some better things, or if experience had weakened their reasons. Yearly there came something to light whereby the Mathematics, Physic, and Magic (for in those are they of Fez most skilful) were amended. There is now-a-days no want of learned men in Germany, Magicians, Cabalists, Physicians, and Philosophers, were there but more love and kindness among them, or that the most part of them would not keep their secrets close only to themselves.

At Fez he did get acquaintance with those which are commonly called the Elementary inhabitants, who revealed unto him many of their secrets, as we Germans likewise might gather together many things if there were the like unity and desire of searching out secrets amongst us.

Of these of Fez he often did confess, that their Magia was not altogether pure, and also that their Cabala was defiled with their Religion; but, notwithstanding, he knew how to make good use of the same, and found still more better grounds for his faith, altogether agreeable with the harmony of the whole world, and wonderfully impressed in all periods of time. Thence proceeded that fair Concord, that as in every several kernel is contained a whole good tree or fruit, so likewise is included in the little body of man, the whole great world, whose religion, policy, health, members, nature, language, words, and works, are agreeing, sympathizing, and in equal tune and melody with God, Heaven, and Earth; and that which is disagreeing with them is error, falsehood, and of the devil, who alone is the first, middle, and last cause of strife, blindness, and darkness in the world. Also, might one examine all and several persons upon the earth, he should find that which is good and right is always agreeing with itself, but all the rest is spotted with a thousand erroneous conceits.

After two years Brother R. C. departed the city Fez, and sailed with many costly things into Spain, hoping well, as he himself had so well and profitably spent his time in his travel, that the learned in Europe would highly rejoice with him, and begin to rule and order all their studies according to those sure and sound foundations. He therefore conferred with the learned in Spain, showing unto them the errors of our arts, and how they might be corrected, and from whence they should gather the true *Inditia* of the times to come, and wherein they ought to agree with those things that are past; also how the faults of the Church and the whole *Philosophia Moralis* were to be amended. He showed them new growths, new fruits, and beasts, which did concord with old philosophy, and prescribed them new Axiomata, whereby all things might fully be restored. But it was to them a laughing matter, and being a new thing unto them, they feared that their great name would be lessened if they should now again begin to learn, and acknowledge their many years' errors, to which they were accustomed, and wherewith they had gained them enough. Who so loveth unquietness, let him be reformed (they said). The same song was also sung to him by other nations, the which moved him the more because it happened to him contrary to his expectation, being then ready bountifully to impart all his arts and secrets to the learned, if they would have but undertaken to write the true and infallible Axiomata, out of all faculties, sciences, and arts, and whole nature, as that which he knew would direct them, like a globe or circle, to the only middle point and *Centrum,* and (as it is usual among the Arabians) it should only serve to the wise and learned for a rule, that also there might be a society in Europe which might have gold, silver, and precious stones, sufficient for to bestow them on kings for their necessary uses and lawful purposes, with which [society] such as be governors might be brought up for to learn all that which God hath suffered man to know, and thereby to be enabled in all times of need to give their counsel unto those that seek it, like the Heathen Oracles.

Verily we must confess that the world in those days was already big with those great commotions, laboring to be delivered of them, and did bring forth painful, worthy men, who brake with all force through darkness and barbarism, and left us who succeeded to follow them. Assuredly, they have been the uppermost point in *Trygono igneo,* whose flame now should be more and more brighter, and shall undoubtedly give to the world the last light.

Such a one likewise hath Theophrastus been in vocation and callings, although he was none of our Fraternity, yet, nevertheless hath he diligently read over the Book M, whereby his sharp ingenious was exalted; but this man was also hindered in his course by the multitude of the learned and wise-seeming men, that he was never able peaceably to confer with others of the knowledge and understanding he had of Nature. And therefore in his writings he rather mocked these busy bodies, and doth not show them altogether what he was; yet, nevertheless, there is found with him well grounded the afore-named Harmonia, which without doubt he had imparted to the learned, if he had not found them rather worthy of subtle vexation then to be instructed in greater arts and sciences. He thus with a free and careless life lost his time, and left unto the world their foolish pleasures.

But that we do not forget our loving Father, Brother C. R., he after many painful travels, and his fruitless true instructions, returned into Germany, which he heartily loved, because of the alterations, which were shortly to come, and of the strange and dangerous contentions. There, although he could have bragged with his art, but specially of the transmutations of metals, yet did he esteem more Heaven, and men, the citizens thereof, than all vain glory and pomp.

Nevertheless, he builded a fitting and neat habitation, in which he ruminated his voyage and philosophy, and reduced them together in a true memorial. In this house he spent a great time in the mathematics, and made many fine instruments, *ex omnibus hujus artis partibus,* whereof there is but little remaining to us, as hereafter you shall understand.

After five years came again into his mind the wished for Reformation; and in regard [of it] he doubted of the aid and help of others, although he himself was painful, lusty, and unwearisom; howsoever he undertook, with some few adjoined with him, to attempt the same. Wherefore he desired to that end to have out of his first cloister (to the which he bare a great affection) three of his brethren, Brother G. V., Brother I. A., and Brother I. O., who had some more knowledge of the arts than at that time many others had. He did bind those three unto himself, to be faithful, diligent, and secret, as also to commit carefully to writing all that which he should direct and instruct them in, to the end that those which were to come, and through especial revelation should be received into this Fraternity, might not be deceived of the least syllable and word.

After this manner began the Fraternity of the Rosie Cross—first, by four persons only, and by them was made the magical language and writing, with a large dictionary, which we yet daily use to God's praise and glory, and do find great wisdom therein. They made also the first part of the Book M, but in respect that that labor was too heavy, and the unspeakable concourse of the sick hindered them, and also whilst his new building (called *Sancti Spiritus*) was now finished, they concluded to draw and receive yet others more into their Fraternity. To this end was chosen Brother R. C., his deceased father's brother's son; Brother B., a skilful painter; G. G., and P. D., their secretary, all Germains except I. A., so in all they were eight in number, all bachelors and of vowed virginity, by whom was collected a book or volume of all that which man can desire, wish, or hope for.

Although we do now freely confess that the world is much amended within a hundred years, yet we are assured that our Axiomata shall immovably remain unto the world's end, also the world in her highest and last age shall not attain to see anything else; for our ROTA takes her beginning from that day when God spoke *Fiat* and shall end when he shall speak *Pereat;* yet God's clock striketh every minute, where ours scarce striketh perfect hours. We also steadfastly believe, that if our Brethren and Fathers had lived in this our present and clear light, they would more roughly have handled the Pope, Mahomet, scribes, artists, and sophisters, and showed themselves more helpful, not simply with sighs and wishing of their end and consummation.

When now these eight Brethren had disposed and ordered all things in such manner, as there was not now need of any great labor, and also that every one was sufficiently instructed and able perfectly to discourse of secret and manifest philosophy, they would not remain any longer together, but, as in the beginning they had agreed, they separated themselves into several countries, because that not only their Axiomata might in secret be more profoundly examined by the learned, but that they if in some country or other they observed anything, or perceived some error, might inform one another of it.

Their agreement was this:—

First, That none of them should profess any other thing then to cure the sick and that gratis.

Second, None of the posterity should be constrained to wear one certain kind of habit, but therein to follow the custom of the country.

Third, That every year, upon the day C., they should meet together at the house *Sancti Spirits,* or write the cause of his absence.

Fourth, Every Brother should look about for a worthy person who, after his decease, might succeed him.

Fifth, The word R. C. should be their seal, mark, and character.

Sixth, The Fraternity should remain secret one hundred years.

These six articles they bound themselves one to another to keep; five of the Brethren departed, only the Brethren B. and D. remained with the Father, Brother R. C., a whole year. When these likewise departed, and then remained by him his cousin and Brother I. O., so that he hath all the days of his life with him two of his Brethren. And although that as yet the Church was not cleansed, nevertheless, we know that they did think of her, and what with longing desire they looked for. Every year they assembled together with joy, and made a full resolution of that which they had done. There must certainly have been great pleasure to hear truly and without invention related and rehearsed all the wonders which God hath poured out here and there throughout the world. Every one may hold it out for certain, that such persons as were sent, and joined together by God and the Heavens, and chosen out of the wisest of men as have lived in many ages, did live together above all others in highest unity, greatest secrecy, and most kindness one towards another.

After such a most laudable sort they did spend their lives, but although they were free from all diseases and pain, yet, notwithstanding, they could not live and pass their time appointed of God. The first of this Fraternity which dyed, and that in England, was I. O., as Brother C. long before had foretold him; he was very expert, and well learned in Cabala, as his Book called H witnesseth. In England, he is much spoken of and chiefly because he cured a young Earl of Norfolk of the leprosy. They had concluded, that, as much as possibly could be, their burial place should be kept secret, as at this day it is not known unto us what is become of some of them, yet every one's place was supplied with a fit successor. But this we will confess publicly by these presents, to the honor of God, that what secret sever we have learned out of the book M, although before our eyes we behold the image and pattern of all the world, yet are there not shown unto us our misfortunes, nor hour of death, the which only is known to God Himself, who thereby would have us keep in a continual readiness. But hereof more in our Confession, where we do set down thirty-seven reasons wherefore we now do make known our Fraternity, and proffer such high mysteries freely, without constraint and reward. Also we do promise more gold then both the Indies bring to the King of Spain, for Europe is with child, and will bring forth a strong child, who shall stand in need of a great godfather's gift.

After the death of I. O., Brother R. C. rested not, but, as soon as he could, called the rest together, and then, as we suppose, his grave was made, although hitherto we (who were the latest) did not know when our loving Father R. C. died, and had no more but the bare names of the beginners, and all their successors to us. Yet there came into our memory a secret, which, through dark and hidden words and speeches of the hundred years, Brother A., the successor of D. (who was of the last and second row of succession, and had lived amongst many of us), did impart unto us of the third row and succession; otherwise we must confess, that after the death of the said A., none of us had in any manner known anything of Brother C. R., and of his first fellow-brethren, then that which was extant of them in our philosophical BIBLIOTHECA, amongst which our AXIOMATA was held for the chiefest, ROTA MUNDI for the most artificial, and PROTHEUS for the most profitable. Likewise, we do not certainly know if these of the second row have been of like wisdom as the first, and if they were admitted to all things.

It shall be declared hereafter to the gentle reader not only what we have heard of the burial of Brother R. C., but also it shall be made manifest publicly, by the foresight, sufferance, and commandment of God, whom we most faithfully obey, that if we shall be answered discreetly and Christian-like, we will not be ashamed to set forth publicly in print our names and surnames, our meetings, or anything else that may be required at our hands.

Now, the true and fundamental relation of the finding out of the high-illuminated man of God, *Fra: C. R. C.,* is this:— After that A. in *Gallia Narbonensi* was deceased, there succeeded in his place our loving Brother N. N. This man, after he had repaired unto us to take the solemn oath of fidelity and secrecy, informed us *bona fide,* that A. had comforted him in telling him, that this Fraternity should ere long not remain so hidden, but should be to the whole German nation helpful, needful, and commendable, of which he was not in anywise in his estate ashamed. The year following, after he had performed his school right, and was minded now to travel, being for that purpose sufficiently provided with Fortunatus' purse, he thought (he being a good architect) to alter something of his building, and to make it more fit. In such renewing, he lighted upon the Memorial Table, which was cast of brass, and contained all the names of the Brethren, with some few other things. This he would transfer into another more fitting vault, for where or when Brother R. C. died, or in what country he was buried, was by our predecessors concealed and unknown unto us. In this table stuck a great nail somewhat strong, so that when it was with force drawn out it took with it an indifferent big stone out of the thin wall or plastering of the hidden door, and so unlooked for uncovered the door, whereat we did with joy and longing throw down the rest of the wall and cleared the door, upon which was written in great letters—

Post CXX Annos Patebo,

With the year of the Lord under it. Therefore we gave God thanks, and let it rest that same night, because first we would overlook our *Rota*—but we refer ourselves again to the Confession, for what we here publish is done for the help of those that are worthy, but to the unworthy, God willing, it will be small profit. For like as our door was after so many years wonderfully discovered, also there shall be opened a door to Europe (when the wall is removed), which already doth begin to appear, and with great desire is expected of many.

In the morning following we opened the door, and there appeared to our sight a vault of seven sides and seven corners, every side five foot broad, and the height of eight foot. Although the sun never shined in this vault, nevertheless, it was enlightened with another sun, which had learned this from the sun, and was situated in the upper part in the center of the ceiling. In the midst, instead of a tomb-stone, was a round altar, covered with a plate of brass, and thereon this engraven:—

A. C. R. C. *Hoc universi compendium unius mihi sepulchrum feci.*

Round about the first circle or brim stood,

Jesus mihi omnia.

In the middle were four figures, inclosed in circles, whose circumscription was,

1. *Nequaquam Vacuum.*
2. *Legis Jugum.*
3. *Libertas Evangelii.*
4. *Dei Gloria Intacta.*

This is all clear and bright, as also the seventh side and the two heptagons. So we kneeled down altogether, and gave thanks to the sole wise, sole mighty, and sole eternal God, who hath taught us more than all men's wits could have found out, praised be His holy name. This vault we parted in three parts, the upper part or ceiling, the wall or side, the ground or floor. Of the upper part you shall understand no more at this time but that it was divided according to the seven sides in the triangle which was in the bright center; but what therein is contained you (that are desirous of our Society) shall, God willing, behold the same with your own eyes. Every side or wall is parted into ten squares, every one with their several figures and sentences, as they are truly showed and set forth *concentrated* here in our book. The bottom again is parted in the triangle, but because therein is described the power and rule of the Inferior Governors, we leave to manifest the same, for fear of the abuse by the evil and ungodly world. But those that are provided and stored with the Heavenly Antidote, do without fear or hurt, tread on and bruise the head of the old and evil serpent, which this our age is well fitted for. Every side or wall had a door for a chest, wherein there lay diverse things, especially all our books, which otherwise we had, besides the *Vocabulary* of Theophrastus Paracelsus of Hohenheim, and these which daily unfalsified we do participate. Herein also, we found his *Itineraries* and *Vita,* whence this relation for the most part is taken. In another chest were looking-glasses of divers virtues, as also in other places were little bells, burning lamps, and chiefly wonderful artificial songs—generally all was done to that end, that if it should happen, after many hundred years, the Fraternity should come to nothing, they might by this only vault be restored again.

Now, as we had not yet seen the dead body of our careful and wise Father, we therefore removed the altar aside; then we lifted up a strong plate of brass, and found a fair and worthy body, whole and unconsumed, as the same is here lively counterfeited,[1] with all the ornaments and attires. In his hand he held a parchment called T,[2]

---

[1] The illustration which is here referred to is, singularly enough, not reproduced in the text of the translation, and it is also absent from the Dutch version of 1617. As there are no other editions of the "Fama Fraternitatis" in the Library of the British Museum, I also am unable to gratify the curiosity of my readers by a copy of the original engraving.

[2] In the English translation the letter I, has been substituted by a typographical error, or by an error of transcription for the T, which is found in all the German editions.

which next unto the Bible is our greatest treasure, which ought not to be delivered to the censure of the world. At the end of this book standeth this following *Elogium*.

Granum pectori Jesu insitum.

C. R. C. ex nobili atque splendida Germaniæ R. C. familia oriundus, vir sui seculi divinis revelationibus, subtilissimis imaginationibus, indefessis laboribus ad cœlestia atque humana mysteria; arcanavè admissus postquam suam (quam Arabico at Africano itineribus collejerat) plus quam regiam, atque imperatoriam Gazam suo seculo nondum convenientem, posteritati eruendam custodivisset et jam suarum Artium, ut et nominis, fides ac conjunctissimos heredes instituisset, mundum minutum omnibus motibus magno illi respondentem fabricasset hocque tandem preteritarum, præsentium, et futurarum, rerum compendio extracto, centenario major, non morbo (quem ipse nunquam corpore expertus erat, nunquam alios infestare sinebat) ullo pellente sed Spiritis Dei evocante, illuminatam animam (inter Fratrum amplexus et ultima oscula) fidelissimo Creatori Deo reddidisset, Pater delictissimus, Frater suavissimus, præceptor fidelissimus, amicus integerimus, a suis ad 120 annos hic absconditus est.

Underneath they had subscribed themselves,
1. *Fra.* I. A. *Fra.* C. H. *electione Fraternitatis caput.*
2. *Fra.* G. V. M. P. C.
3. *Fra.* F. R. C., *Junior hœres S. Spirits.*
4. *Fra.* F. B. M. P. A., *Pictor et Architectus.*
5. *Fra.* G. G. M. P. I., *Cabalista.*

Secundi Circuli.

1. *Fra.* P. A. *Successor, Fra.* I. O., *Mathematicus.*
2. *Fra.* A. *Successor, Fra.* P. D.

3. *Fra. R. Successor Patris* C. R. C., *cum Christo triumphantis.*

At the end was written,

Ex Deo nascimur, in Jesu morimur, per Spiritum Sanctum reviviscimus.

At that time was already dead; Brother I. O. and Brother D., but their burial places where is it to be found? We doubt not but our *Fra. Senior* hath the same, and some especial thing laid in earth, and perhaps likewise hidden. We also hope that this our example will stir up others more diligently to enquire after their names (which we have therefore published), and to search for the place of their burial; the most part of them, by reason of their practice and physic, are yet known and praised among very old folks; so might perhaps our GAZA be enlarged, or, at least, be better cleared.

Concerning *Minutum Mundum,* we found it kept in another little altar, truly more finer then can be imagined by any understanding man, but we will leave him undescribed until we shall be truly answered upon this our true-hearted FAMA. So we have covered it again with the plates, and set the altar thereon, shut the door and made it sure with all our seals. Moreover, by instruction, and command of our ROTA, there are come to sight some books, among which is contained M (which were made instead of household care by the praiseworthy M. P.). Finally, we departed the one from the other, and left the natural heirs in possession of our jewels. And so we do expect the answer and judgment of the learned and unlearned.

Howbeit we know after a time there will now be a general reformation, both of divine and humane things, according to our desire and the expectation of others; for it is fitting that before the rising of the Sun there should appear and break forth *Aurora,* or some clearness, or divine light in the sky. And so, in the meantime, some few, which shall give their names, may join together, thereby to increase the number and respect of our Fraternity, and make a happy and wished for beginning of our PHILOSOPHICAL CANONS, prescribed to us by our Brother R. C., and be partakers with us of our treasures (which never can fail or be wasted) in all humility and love, to be eased of this world's labors, and not walk so blindly in the knowledge of the wonderful works of God.

But that also every Christian may know of what Religion and belief we are, we confess to have the knowledge of Jesus Christ (as the same now in these last days, and chiefly in Germany, most clear and pure is professed, and is now a days cleansed and void of all swerving people, heretics, and false prophets), in certain and noted countries maintained, defended, and propagated. In addition, we use two Sacraments, as they are instituted with all Forms and Ceremonies of the first and renewed Church. In *Politia* we acknowledge the Roman Empire and *Quartam Monarchiam* for our Christian head, albeit we know what alterations be at hand, and would fain impart the same with all our hearts to other godly learned men, notwithstanding our handwriting which is in our hands, no man (except God alone) can make it common, nor any unworthy person is able to bereave us of it. But we shall help with secret aid this so good a cause, as God shall permit or hinder us. For our God is not blind, as the heathen's Fortuna, but is the Churches' ornament and the honor of the Temple. Our Philosophy also is not a new invention, but as Adam after his fall hath received it, and as Moses and Solomon used it, also it ought not much to be doubted of, or contradicted by other opinions, or meanings; but seeing the truth is peaceable, brief, and always like herself in all things, and especially accorded by with *Jesus in omni parte* and all members, and as He is the true image of the Father, so is she His image, so it shall not be said, This is true according to Philosophy, but true according to Theology; and wherein Plato, Aristotle, Pythagoras, and others did hit the mark, and wherein Enoch, Abraham, Moses, Solomon, did excel, but especially wherewith that wonderful book the Bible agreeth. All that same concurreth together, and maketh a sphere or globe whose total parts are equidistant from the center, as hereof more at large and more plain shall be spoken of in Christianly Conference (in den Boecke des Levens).

But now concerning, and chiefly in this our age, the ungodly and accursed gold-making, which hath gotten so much the upper hand, whereby under color of it, many runagates and roguish people do use great villainies, and cozen and abuse the credit which is given them; yea, now a days men of discretion do hold the transmutation of metals to be the highest point and *fastigium* in philosophy. This is all their intent and desire, and that God would be most esteemed by them and honored which could make great store of gold, the which with unpremeditated prayers they hope to obtain of the all-knowing God and searcher of all hearts; but we by these presents publicly testify, that the true philosophers are far of another mind, esteeming little the making of gold, which is but a *paragon,* for besides that they have a thousand better things. We say with our loving Father

C. R. C., *Phy. aurium nisi quantum aurum,* for unto him the whole nature is detected; he doth not rejoice that he can make gold, and that, as saith Christ, the devils are obedient unto him, but is glad that he seeth the Heavens open, the angels of God ascending and descending, and his name written in the book of life.

Also we do testify that, under the name of *Chymia,* many books and pictures are set forth in *Contumeliam gloriæ Dei,* as we will name them in their due season, and will give to the pure-hearted a catalogue or register of them. We pray all learned men to take heed of these kinds of books, for the Enemy never rested, but sowed his weeds until a stronger one doth root them out.

So, according to the will and meaning of *Fra.* C. R. C., we his brethren request again all the learned in Europe who shall read (sent forth in five languages) this our *Fama* and *Confessio,* that it would please them with good deliberation to ponder this our offer, and to examine most nearly and sharply their arts, and behold the present time with all diligence, and to declare their mind, either *communicato consilio,* or *singulatim* by print. And although at this time we make no mention either of our names or meetings, yet nevertheless every one's opinion shall assuredly come to our hands, in what language so ever it be, nor any body shall fail, who so gives but his name, to speak with some of us, either by word of mouth, or else, if there be some left, in writing. And this we say for a truth, that whosoever shall earnestly, and from his heart, bear affection unto us, it shall be beneficial to him in goods, body, and soul; but he that is false-hearted, or only greedy of riches, the same first of all shall not be able in any manner of wise to hurt us, but bring him to utter ruin and destruction. In addition, our building, although one hundred thousand people had very near seen and beheld the same, shall for ever remain untouched, undestroyed, and hidden to the wicked world.

Sub umbra alarum tuarum, Jehova.

CHAPTER II.

THE CONFESSION OF THE ROSICRUCIAN FRATERNITY, ADDRESSED TO THE LEARNED OF EUROPE.

THE translation of this manifesto which follows the Fama in the edition accredited by the great name of Eugenius Philalethes is prolix and careless: being made not from the Latin original but from the later German version. As a relic of English Rosicrucian literature I have wished to preserve it, and having subjected it to a searching revision throughout, it now represents the original with sufficient fidelity for all practical purposes. The "Confessio Fraternitatis" appeared in the year 1615 in a Latin work entitled "Secretioris Philosophiæ Consideratio Brevio à Philippo à Gabella, Philosophiæ studioso, conscripta; et nunc primum unà cum Confessione Fraternitatis R. C.," in lucem edita, Cassellis, excudebat G. Wesselius, a 1615. Quarto." It was prefaced by the following advertisement:—

"Here, gentle reader, you shall find incorporated in our Confession thirty-seven reasons of our purpose and intention, the which according to thy pleasure thou may seek out and compare together, considering within thyself if they be sufficient to allure thee. Verily, it requires no small pains to induce any one to believe what doth not yet appear, but when it shall be revealed in the full blaze of day, I suppose we should be ashamed of such questionings. And as we do now securely call the Pope Antichrist, which was formerly a capital offence in every place, so we know certainly that what we here keep secret we shall in the future thunder forth with uplifted voice, the which, reader, with us desire with all thy heart that it may happen most speedily. "FRATRES R. C."

Confessio Fraternitatis R. C. ad Eruditos Europœ.

CHAPTER I.

Whatsoever you have heard, O mortals, concerning our Fraternity by the trumpet sound of the Fama R. C., do not either believe it hastily, or willfully suspect it. It is Jehovah, who seeing how the world is falling to decay, and near to its end, doth hasten it again to its beginning, inverting the course of Nature, and so what heretofore hath been sought with great pains and daily labor He doth lay open now to those thinking of no such thing, offering it to the willing and thrusting it on the reluctant, that it may become to the good that which will smooth the troubles of human life and break the violence of unexpected blows of Fortune, but to the ungodly that which will augment their sins and their punishments.

Although we believe ourselves to have sufficiently unfolded to you in the *Fama* the nature of our order, wherein we follow the will of our most excellent father, nor can by any be suspected of heresy, nor of any attempt against the commonwealth, we hereby do condemn the East and the West (meaning the Pope and Mahomet) for their blasphemies against our Lord Jesus Christ, and offer to the chief head of the Roman Empire our prayers, secrets, and great treasures of gold. Yet we have thought well for the sake of the learned to add somewhat more to this, and make a better explanation, if there be anything too deep, hidden, and set down over dark, in the Fama, or for certain reasons altogether omitted, whereby we hope the learned will be more addicted unto us, and easier to approve our counsel.

CHAPTER II.

Concerning the amendment of philosophy, we have (as much as at this present is needful) declared that the same is altogether weak and faulty; nay, whilst many (I know not how) allege that she is sound and strong, to us it is certain that she fetches her last breath.

But as commonly even in the same place where there break forth a new disease, nature discovered a remedy against the same, so amidst so many infirmities of philosophy there do appear the right means, and unto our Fatherland sufficiently offered, whereby she may become sound again, and new or renovated may appear to a renovated world.

No other philosophy we have then that which is the head of all the faculties, sciences, and arts, the which (if we behold our age) contained much of Theology and Medicine, but little of Jurisprudence; which searched heaven and earth with exquisite analysis, or, to speak briefly thereof, which doth sufficiently manifest the Microsmus man, whereof if some of the more orderly in the number of the learned shall respond to our fraternal invitation, they shall find among us far other and greater wonders then those they heretofore did believe, marvel at, and profess.

CHAPTER III.

Wherefore, to declare briefly our meaning hereof, it becomes us to labor carefully that the surprise of our challenge may be taken from you, to show plainly that such secrets are not lightly esteemed by us, and not to spread an opinion abroad among the vulgar that the story concerning them is a foolish thing. For it is not absurd to suppose many are overwhelmed with the conflict of thought which is occasioned by our unhoped graciousness, unto whom (as yet) be unknown the wonders of the sixth age, or who, by reason of the course of the world, esteem the things to come like unto the present, and, hindered by the obstacles of their age, live no otherwise in the world then as men blind, who, in the light of noon, discern nothing only by feeling.

CHAPTER IV.

Now concerning the first part, we hold that the meditations of our Christian father on all subjects which from the creation of the world have been invented, brought forth, and propagated by human ingenuity, through God's revelation, or through the service of Angels or spirits, or through the sagacity of understanding, or through the experience of long observation, are so great, that if all books should perish, and by God's almighty sufferance all writings and all learning should be lost, yet posterity will be able thereby to lay a new foundation of sciences, and to erect a new citadel of truth; the which perhaps would not be so hard to do as if one should begin to pull down and destroy the old, ruinous building, then enlarge the fore-court, afterwards bring light into the private chambers, and then change the doors, staples, and other things according to our intention.

Therefore, it must not be expected that new comers shall

attain at once all our weighty secrets. They must proceed step by step from the smaller to the greater, and must not be retarded by difficulties.

Wherefore should we not freely acquiesce in the only truth then seek through so many windings and labyrinths, if only it had pleased God to lighten unto us the sixth Candelabrum? Was it not sufficient for us to fear neither hunger, poverty, diseases, nor age? Was it not an excellent thing to live always so as if you had lived from the beginning of the world, and should still live to the end thereof? So to live in one place that neither the people, who dwell beyond the Ganges, could hide anything, nor those, which live in Peru, might be able to keep secret their counsels from thee? So to read in one only book as to discern, understand, and remember whatsoever in all other books (which heretofore have been, are now, and hereafter shall come out) hath been, is, and shall be learned out of them? So to sing or to play that instead of stony rocks you could draw pearls, instead of wild beast's spirits, and instead of Pluto, you could soften the mighty princes of the world? O mortals, diverse is the counsel of God and your convenience, Who hath decreed at this time to increase and enlarge the number of our Fraternity, the which we with such joy have undertaken, as we have heretofore obtained this great treasure without our merits, yea, without any hope or expectation; the same we purpose with such fidelity to put in practice, that neither compassion nor pity for our own children (which some of us in the Fraternity have) shall move us, since we know that these unhoped for good things cannot be inherited, nor be conferred promiscuously.

CHAPTER V.

If there be any body now which on the other side will complain of our discretion, that we offer our treasures so freely and indiscriminately, and do not rather regard more the godly, wise, or princely persons then the common people, with him we are in no wise angry (for the accusation is not without moment), but with all we affirm that we have by no means made common property of our arcana, albeit they resound in five languages within the ears of the vulgar, both because, as we well know, they will not move gross wits, and because the worth of those who shall be accepted into our Fraternity will not be measured by their curiosity, but by the rule and pattern of our revelations. A thousand times the unworthy may clamor, a thousand times may present themselves, yet God hath commanded our ears that they should hear none of them, and hath so compassed us about with His clouds that unto us, His servants, no violence can be done; wherefore now no longer are we beheld by human eyes, unless they have received strength borrowed from the eagle.

For the rest, it hath been necessary that the Fama should be set forth in everyone's mother tongue, lest those should not be defrauded of the knowledge thereof, whom (although they be unlearned) God hath not excluded from the happiness of this Fraternity, which is divided into degrees; as those which dwell in Damcar, who have a far different politick order from the other Arabians; for there do govern only understanding men, who, by the king's permission, make particular laws, according unto which example the government shall also be instituted in Europe (according to the description set down by our Christianly Father), when that shall come to pass which must precede, when our Trumpet shall resound with full voice and with no prevarications of meaning, when, namely, those things of which a few now whisper and darken with enigmas, shall openly fill the earth, even as after many secret chafing of pious people against the pope's tyranny, and after timid reproof, he with great violence and by a great onset was cast down from his seat and abundantly trodden under foot, whose final fall is reserved for an age when he shall be torn in pieces with nails, and a final groan shall end his ass's braying, the which, as we know, is already manifest to many learned men in Germany, as their tokens and secret congratulations bear witness.

CHAPTER VI.

We could here relate and declare what all the time from the year 1378 (when our Christian father was born) till now hath happened, what alterations he hath seen in the world these one hundred and six years of his life, what he left after his happy death to be attempted by our Fathers and by us, but brevity, which we do observe, will not permit at this present to make rehearsal of it; it is enough for those which do not despise our declaration to have touched upon it, thereby to prepare the way for their more close union and association with us. Truly, to whom it is permitted to behold, read, and thenceforward teach himself those great characters which the Lord God hath inscribed upon the world's mechanism, and which He repeats through the mutations of Empires, such an one is already ours, though as yet unknown to himself; and as we know he will not neglect our invitation, so, in like manner, we abjure all deceit, for we promise that no man's uprightness and hopes shall deceive him who shall make himself known to us under the seal of secrecy and desire our familiarity. But to the false and to impostors, and to those who seek other things then wisdom, we witness by these presents pub likely, we cannot be betrayed unto them to our hurt, nor be known to them without the will of God, but they shall certainly be partakers of that terrible commination spoken of in our *Fama*, and their impious designs shall fall back upon their own heads, while our treasures shall remain untouched, till the Lion shall arise and exact them as his right, receive and employ them for the establishment of his kingdom.

CHAPTER VII.

One thing should here, O mortals, be established by us, that God hath decreed to the world before her end, which presently thereupon shall ensue, an influx of truth, light, and grandeur, such as he commanded should accompany Adam from Paradise and sweeten the misery of man: Wherefore there shall cease all falsehood, darkness, and bondage, which little by little, with the great globe's revolution, hath crept into the arts, works, and governments of men, darkening the greater part of them. Thence hath proceeded that innumerable diversity of persuasions, falsities, and heresies, which makes choice difficult to the wisest men, seeing on the one part they were hindered by the reputation of philosophers and on the other by the facts of experience, which if (as we trust) it can be once removed, and instead thereof a single and self-same rule be instituted, then there will indeed remain thanks unto them which have taken pains therein, but the sum of the so great work shall be attributed to the blessedness of our age.

As we now confess that many high intelligences by their writings will be a great furtherance unto this Reformation which is to come, so do we by no means arrogate to ourselves this glory, as if such a work were only imposed on us, but we testify with our Savior Christ, that sooner shall the stones rise up and offer their service, then there shall be any want of executors of God's counsel.

CHAPTER VIII.

God, indeed, hath already sent messengers which should testify His will, to wit, some new stars which have appeared in *Serpentarius* and *Cygnus,* the which powerful signs of a great Council show forth how for all things which human ingenuity discovers, God calls upon His hidden knowledge, as likewise the Book of Nature, though it stands open truly for all eyes, can be read or understood by only a very few.

As in the human head there are two organs of hearing, two of sight, and two of smell, but only one of speech, and it were but vain to expect speech from the ears, or hearing from the eyes, so there have been ages which have seen, others which have heard, others again that have smelt and tasted. Now, there remains that in a short and swiftly approaching time honor should be likewise given to the tongue, that what formerly saw, heard, and smelt shall finally speak, after the world shall have slept away the intoxication of her poisoned and stupefying chalice, and with an open heart, bare head, and naked feet shall merrily and joyfully go forth to meet the sun rising in the morning.

CHAPTER IX.

These characters and letters, as God hath here and there incorporated them in the Sacred Scriptures, so hath He imprinted them most manifestly on the wonderful work of creation, on the heavens, the earth, and on all beasts, so that as the mathematician predicts eclipses, so we prognosticate the obscurations of the church, and how long they shall last. From these letters we have borrowed our magic writing, and thence have made for ourselves a new language, in which the nature of things is expressed, so that it is no wonder that we are not so eloquent in other tongues, least of all in this Latin, which we know to be by no means in agreement with that of Adam and of Enoch, but to have been contaminated by the confusion of Babel.[1]

CHAPTER X.

But this also must by no means be omitted, that, while there are yet some eagle's feathers in our way, the which do hinder our purpose, we do exhort to the sole, only, assiduous, and continual study of the Sacred Scriptures, for he that take all his pleasures therein shall know that he hath prepared for himself an excellent way to come into our Fraternity, for this is the whole sum of our Laws, that as there is not a character in that great miracle of the world which has not a claim on the memory, so those are nearest and likes unto us who do make the Bible the rule of their life, the end of all their studies, and the compendium of the universal world, from whom we require not that it should be continually in their mouth, but that they should appropriately apply

---

[1] The original reads *Babylonis confusione,* "by the confusion of Babylon."

its true interpretation to all ages of the world, for it is not our custom so to debase the divine oracle, that while there are innumerable expounders of the same, some adhere to the opinions of their party, some make sport of Scripture as if it were a tablet of wax to be indifferently made use of by theologians, philosophers, doctors, and mathematicians. Be it ours rather to bear witness, that from the beginning of the world there hath not been given to man a more excellent, admirable, and wholesome book then the Holy Bible; Blessed is he who possesses it, more blessed is he who reads it, most blessed of all is he who truly understand it, while he is most like to God who both understands and obeys it.

CHAPTER XI.

Now, whatsoever hath been said in the Fama, through hatred of impostors, against the transmutation of metals and the supreme medicine of the world, we desire to be so understood, that this so great gift of God we do in no manner set at naught, but as it bring not always with it the knowledge of Nature, while this knowledge brunet forth both that and an infinite number of other natural miracles, it is right that we be rather earnest to attain to the knowledge of philosophy, nor tempt excellent wits to the tincture of metals sooner then to the observation of Nature. He must needs be insatiable to whom neither poverty, diseases, nor danger can any longer reach, who, as one raised above all men, hath rule over that which doth anguish, afflict, and pain others, yet will give himself again to idle things, will build, make wars, and domineer, because he hath of gold sufficient, and of silver an inexhaustible fountain. God judges far otherwise, who exalted the lowly, and castes the proud into obscurity; to the silent he send his angels to hold speech with them, but the babblers he drives into the wilderness, which is the judgment due to the Roman impostor who now poured his blasphemies with open mouth against Christ, nor yet in the full light, by which Germany hath detected his caves and subterranean passages, will abstain from lying, that thereby he may fulfill the measure of his sin, and be found worthy of the axe. Therefore, one day it will come to pass, that the mouth of this viper shall be stopped, and his triple crown shall be brought to naught, of which things more fully when we shall have met together.

CHAPTER XII.

For conclusion of our Confession we must earnestly admonish you, that you cast away, if not all, yet most of the worthless books of pseudo chymists, to whom it is a jest to apply the Most Holy Trinity to vain things, or to deceive men with monstrous symbols and enigmas, or to profit by the curiosity of the credulous; our age doth produce many such, one of the greatest being a stage-player, a man with sufficient ingenuity for imposition; such doth the enemy of human welfare mingle among the good seed, thereby to make the truth more difficult to be believed, which in herself is simple and naked, while falsehood is proud, haughty, and colored with a luster of seeming godly and humane wisdom. Ye that are wise eschew such books, and have recourse to us, who seek not your moneys, but offer unto you most willingly our great treasures. We hunt not after your goods with invented lying tinctures, but desire to make you partakers of our goods. We do not reject parables, but invite you to the clear and simple explanation of all secrets; we seek not to be received of you, but call you unto our more then kingly houses and palaces, by no motion of our own, but (lest you be ignorant of it) as forced thereto by the Spirit of God, commanded by the testament of our most excellent Father, and impelled by the occasion of this present time.

CHAPTER XIII.

What think you, therefore, O Mortals, seeing that we sincerely confess Christ, execrate the pope, addict ourselves to the true philosophy, lead a worthy life, and daily call, entreat, and invite many more unto our Fraternity, unto whom the same Light of God likewise appeared? Consider you not that, having pondered the gifts which are in you, having measured your understanding in the Word of God, and having weighed the imperfection and inconsistencies of all the arts, you may at length in the future deliberate with us upon their remedy, co-operate in the work of God, and be serviceable to the constitution of your time? On which work these profits will follow, that all those goods, which Nature hath dispersed in every part of the earth, shall at one time and altogether be given to you, *tanquam in centro solis et lunæ*. Then shall you be able to expel from the world all those things which darken human knowledge and hinder action, such as the vain (astronomical) epicycles and eccentric circles.

CHAPTER XIV.

You, however, for whom it is enough to be serviceable out of curiosity to any ordinance, or who are dazzled by the glistering of gold, or who, though now upright, might be led away by such unexpected great riches into an effeminate, idle, luxurious, and pompous life, do not disturb our sacred silence by your clamor, but think, that although there be a medicine which might fully cure all diseases, yet those whom God wishes to try or to chastise shall not be abetted by such an opportunity, so that if we were able to enrich and instruct the whole world, and liberate it from innumerable hardships, yet shall we never be manifested unto any man unless God should favor it, yea, it shall be so far from him who thinks to be partaker of our riches against the will of God that he shall sooner lose his life in seeking us, then attain happiness by finding us.

Fraternitas R. C.

Look for these and other great titles at:
http://www.stoneguildpublishing.com

Book of Ancient and Accepted Scottish Rite by Charles T. McClenachan
The Book of the Holy Graal by A. E. Waite
The Book of the Lodge by George Oliver
The Builders by Joseph Fort Newton
Chymical Marriage of Christian Rosencreutz translated by A. E. Waite
The Doctrine and Literature of the Kabalah by A. E. Waite
Fama Fraternitatis and Confession of the Rosicrucians by A. E. Waite
Freemasonry in the Holy Land by Robert Morris
The Freemason's Manual by Jeremiah How
The Freemason's Monitor by Daniel Sickels
The History of Freemasonry and Concordant Orders
The History of Initiation by George Oliver
Illustrations of the Symbols of Freemasonry by Jacob Ernst
The Kybalion by The Three Initiates
Low Twelve by Edward S. Ellis
The New Masonic Trestleboard by Charles W. Moore
Opinions on Speculative Masonry by James C. Odiorne
The Perfect Ceremonies of Craft Masonry
The Poetry of Freemasonry by Rob Morris
Real History of the Rosicrucians by A. E. Waite
The Symbolism of Freemasonry by Albert G. Mackey
Symbolism of the Three Degrees by Oliver Day Street
Taylor's Monitor by William M. Taylor
Taylor-Hamilton Monitor of Symbolic Masonry by Sam R. Hamilton
Three Hundred Masonic Odes and Poems by Rob Morris
True Masonic Chart or Hieroglyphic Monitor by Jeremy Cross

www.ingramcontent.com/pod-product-compliance
Lightning Source LLC
Chambersburg PA
CBHW070520090426
42735CB00012B/2846